Signs and Wonders Revelations

Heaven On Earth

By Bill Vincent

Signs and Wonders Revelations

© 2013 by Bill Vincent.

All rights reserved. No part of this book may be reproduced, stored in a retrieval system or transmitted in any form or by any means without the prior written permission of the publishers, except by a reviewer who may quote brief passages in a review to be printed in a newspaper, magazine or journal.

Softcover 978-1-304-98978-9
Hardcover 978-1-304-98979-6

PUBLISHED BY REVIVAL WAVES OF GLORY BOOKS & PUBLISHING
www.revivalwavesofglory.com
Litchfield, IL

Printed in the United States of America

Signs and Wonders Revelations

Table of Contents

Introduction 4
New Things 7
Feathers From Heaven 12
Gold Nuggets & Fillings 15
Gold Dust & Gold Flakes 18
Glory Oil 25
Restoration of Signs & Wonders 29
Signs Are For Everyone 38
Testimonies 45
About the Author 58
Recommended Books 61

Introduction

Prior to 2008 it was not even possible that I would be sitting down to write about signs and wonders. The reason being is that I didn't even believe in any manifested signs & wonders. I was a Pastor in Litchfield, IL and was invited to a David Herzog meeting. They said to me come on there will be gold dust in the meeting. I responded what is that for. I told them I wanted something tangible from God not some gold dust. Little did I know gold dust was definitely from God?

I have experienced some of the most glorious times in God's Presence. I have seen and have been a sign and wonder. God has shown His awesome wonders to and through me so much that it seems like a dream.

Whether it's gold dust, multi colored dust, gold flakes, gold nuggets, feathers, glory clouds, misting rain, gemstones, diamonds, mounted rings and more. God's Glory can manifest some of the most strange but real signs.

I have been told by some ministers that have experienced signs and wonders that we were blessed greatly to see all that we've seen.
God moved more in this type of manifestations more when it was just a few people. I believe it is because of the unity we had. It takes pressing in unity together for God that brings His Glory and releases His signs and wonders.

We will have full color pictures of signs and wonders that have happened since 2008. We believe and hope you will to. In God's Glory anything can happen.

God wanted me to say this here. You read this book expecting signs and wonders to happen and they will.

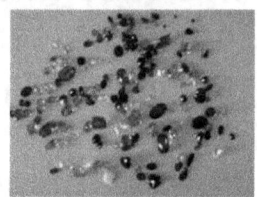

Chapter One

New Things

Over the last twenty years I've heard over and over again God is doing a new thing. You know what, God starts doing new things and every time He does the Church has a problem with it. Most of the Church has been crying out for God to move in awesome signs, wonders and miracles. When God does it, many Christians reject it because of doubt and unbelief.

Doubt and unbelief is something in the modern day Church. God's Word clearly declares signs shall follow them that believe. I find it funny now but there was a time when I was full of doubt and unbelief. God woke me up and I hope everyone comes to the realization that God's Glory is available for everyone.

Luke 7:22, 23 Then Jesus answering said unto them, Go your way, and tell John what things ye have seen and heard; how that the blind see, the lame walk, the lepers are cleansed, the deaf hear, the dead are raised, to the poor the gospel is preached. And blessed is *he,* whosoever shall not be **offended** in me.

After the awesome resurrection of Jesus some did not believe.

Mark 16:11 And they, when they had heard that he was alive, and had been seen of her, **believed not**.

Mark 16:12, 13 After that he appeared in another form unto two of them, as they walked, and went into the country. And they went and told *it* unto the residue: **neither believed they them**.

There is always going to be those who choose not to believe.

Many years ago God began to move in many ways and it was rejected by many.

Many Ministers whom have pioneered the new things were attacked by the Church for it.

Here are some of the things I've seen the Church stand against.

People being slain in the Spirit

Holy laughter

Speaking in tongues

Prophetic ministry

Shaking from the presence of God

People making unusual sounds

At the time when all the things just stated began to happen it was a problem for a lot of Christians. The main reason it was a NEW thing. God is always doing more and more of what I believe is already happening in Heaven. There are angelic visitations, signs and wonders. If it's God I say have Your way God.

Isaiah 43:18, 19 Remember ye not the former things, neither consider the things of old. Behold, **I will do a new thing**; now it shall spring forth; shall ye not know it? I will even make a way in the wilderness, *and* rivers in the desert.

Isaiah 42:9, 10 Behold, the former things are come to pass, and **new things do I declare**: before they spring forth I tell you of them. Sing unto the LORD a new song, *and* his praise from the end of the earth, ye that go down to the sea, and all that is therein; the isles, and the inhabitants thereof.

God says I'm doing a new thing and I take Him at His Word.

Chapter Two

Feathers From Heaven

In the midst of God's Glory especially while talking about angels and heaven feathers fall in the meetings. I know it is unusual for feathers to fall inside of a building.

During the Revival in Litchfield, IL we had feathers in many meetings. They would fall during worship and people would try to catch them. Some of them were caught and others kept moving like they were still attached to an angel. When I would preach and the presence of God would start increasing feathers would fall slowly from the ceiling. There would be one here and two there. Some meetings had a couple and others would have a dozen or more.

There were times my team and I would be sitting around talking about all God was doing and feathers would fall in our midst. There was one time we worshiped for hours and then took a break. We locked the room while we went to eat and came back and there were dozens of feathers all through the sanctuary.

Malachi 4:2 But unto you that fear my name shall the Sun of righteousness arise with **healing in his wings**; and ye shall go forth, and grow up as calves of the stall.

Sometimes I believe that when feathers begin to fall the

atmosphere is charged for healing and miracles.

Some people say they don't believe God would have feathers fall.

Anyone who has seen this awesome phenomena has accepted it. God has many ways He wants to let us know He is in our midst. Feathers are just one of many.

Chapter Three

Gold Nuggets & Fillings

The Bible states that the gold and silver is God's. People can say they don't believe in many of the signs and wonders but it's hard to argue with gold tooth fillings.

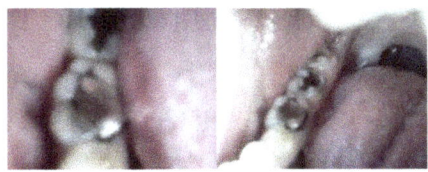

We have had gold nuggets any where from tiny to ten grams fall on the pulpit. Some people tested the gold nuggets and said they were real, some 14K and others 18K.

My question to people who get everything tested is what happens when it doesn't test real. I know for a fact sometimes God will give us a little to see if we receive it before He will give us more.

In the revival we have had some things manifest that were plated and not the best according to our way of thinking. After we received the lesser as a gift from God, He will give us more. In the beginning of the signs and wonders the quality wasn't real or the best we could imagine. After a year straight of God manifesting signs and wonders, we began to have the best gemstones and the best gold fall from Heaven.

We have had some people receive gold and silver in their teeth. A couple showed us ten or more fillings. There were many in the shape of a cross. We even had white fillings. Many times the fillings were changed from the ugly black to beautiful gold. Some dentists have stated that it was a unusual type of gold.

The people who have received this awesome sign from God have been so excited when they tell about it. Sometimes when I have been in meetings God will say, someone is getting a gold filling. After that people will look in each others mouths and someone will scream I have one!

It really stirs the faith in the atmosphere because most of the time it's first time visitors that know it had to be God.

Chapter Four

Gold Dust & Gold Flakes

When God first brought gold flakes to us we thought this has to be glitter from some children. As I said earlier we receive the little and God will give us more.

Late in 2008 we were having Revival in Litchfield, IL and every once and a while there would be a pile of colored dust in one area. We were having some great glory presence and have to say we were all clueless to what was happening. We would find these piles and because we thought it was nothing we would quickly vacuum it up. We were having special meetings one week in the midst of Revival and there started to fall silver flakes all over the foyer.

A few of us were disturbed thinking someone was mocking God by dumping silver. Later after the meetings we were discussing the silver among our team of ministry. I was reminded that God said He was going to begin greeting people in the foyer. Then we began to think could this be God. We began to repent as a group and said God if this is you have your way. After that day within a short time the entire building was covered by glory dust. It was amazing!

Haggai 2:8, 9 The **silver** *is* mine, and the **gold** *is* mine, saith the LORD of hosts. The glory of this latter house shall be greater than of the former, saith the LORD of hosts: and in this place will I give peace, saith the LORD of hosts.

After a while in our meetings gold dust, multi-colored dust began to manifest on the pulpit while I was preaching.

We had piles that everyone began to see pictures formed in the dust. One pile formed the image of Jesus. It was amazing and I wish I had a photo for you to see of it. We had another pile that was a perfect picture of an eagle.

Remember I was preaching to a crowd of people and the piles of glory dust would fall on the pulpit for all to see.

Job 28: 5,6 NKJ As for the earth, from it comes bread, But underneath it is turned up as by fire. Its stones are the source of sapphires, And it contains **gold dust.**

In most services I get gold upon my head and shoulders. There were a couple times that people called me iron man because of the thick gold that covered my face and forehead.

Job 22:24, 25 Then shalt thou lay up **gold as dust**, and the *gold* of Ophir as the stones of the brooks. Yea, the Almighty shall be thy defence, and thou shalt have plenty of silver.

When we had spontaneous worship services God would cover me with glory dust in front of everyone. It was more amazing than words can say. When I tell these stories understand that it is God who does it and I give Him all the Glory.

Psalms 45:13 The king's daughter *is* all glorious within: her clothing *is* of **wrought gold**.

Psalms 68:13 Though ye have lien among the pots, *yet shall ye be as* the **wings of a dove covered with silver, and her feathers with yellow gold**.

Ezekiel 16:10-14 I clothed thee also with broidered work, and shod thee with badgers' skin, and I girded thee about with fine linen, and I covered thee with silk. I decked thee also with ornaments, and I put bracelets upon thy hands, and a chain on thy neck. And I put a jewel on thy forehead, and earrings in thine ears, and a beautiful crown upon thine head. Thus wast thou **decked with gold** and silver; and thy raiment *was of* fine linen, and silk, and broidered work; thou didst eat fine flour, and honey, and oil: and thou wast exceeding beautiful, and thou didst prosper into a kingdom. And thy renown went forth among the heathen for thy beauty: for it *was* perfect through my comeliness, which I had put upon thee, saith the Lord GOD.

The Bible says that the Glory can be seen upon us. How about gold dust upon us, it manifests upon God's people when the presence is there.

Isaiah 60:1, 2 Arise, shine; for thy light is come, and the **glory of the LORD is risen upon thee**. For, behold, the darkness shall cover the earth, and gross darkness the people: but the LORD shall arise upon thee, and **his glory shall be seen upon thee.**

Exodus 34:29 And it came to pass, when Moses came down from mount Sinai with the two tables of testimony in Moses' hand, when he came down from the mount, that Moses wist not that the skin of **his face shone** while he talked with him.

Chapter Five

Glory Oil

One of the greatest manifestations from God was oil. The first time God put sweet smelling oil all over our CD table in the foyer. It was a mess. One thing I want to note that the oil didn't manifest as much. The reason was that people were worried about the stained carpet.

There was one time the front door of our Church was found with oil dripping down it. We had the oil soaked up with old towels and rags. We cut the soaked rags for prayer clothes. We began to hand them out at meetings and received several testimonies. The front door area smelled so awesome for a long time after.

Song of Solomon 5:5 I rose up to open to my beloved; and my hands dropped *with* myrrh, and my fingers *with* sweet smelling myrrh, upon the handles of the lock.

After having meetings all weekend we discovered oil on a Sunday morning. We always locked the sanctuary after meetings because of all the things God was doing. We wanted to keep the purity of the signs. That morning we found that the pulpit was pouring out oil. It was still flowing down. We again had some people soak it up and even filled a couple jars with it. Remember this was the pulpit I had to preach from. I remember I felt presence that morning as I never had before.

Psalms 23:5 Thou preparest a table before me in the presence of mine enemies: thou anointest my head with oil; my cup runneth over.

Once I was preaching on a Sunday morning after having oil appear a few times. It wasn't much but oil began to soak up my sermon and pour off the side of the pulpit. It really was a site to see. The glory level went through the roof and miracles began to happen.

Zechariah 4:12 And I answered again, and said unto him, What *be these* two olive branches which through the two golden pipes empty the **golden** *oil* out of themselves?

Zechariah 4:14 Then said he, These *are* the two anointed ones, that stand by the Lord of the whole earth.

One thing I want to note it isn't just signs and wonders. It is also healings, miracles and wonderful presence. When signs and wonders show up it is just a sign God is in your midst. When God shows up anything can happen.

Chapter Six

Restoration of Signs & Wonders

I believe one of the things that is happening right now is, God is restoring what was lost even since the foundation of the world. There is a restoration of things even from the Garden of Eden.

One of the greatest manifestations from God is gemstones. We have had thousands of gemstones since 2008.

God has blessed us with some of the largest gemstones in history. We had a 1200 ct opaque Emerald fall on the pulpit during a meeting. Everyone heard that one. It was ice cold too.

There were times we would get a few nice gemstones and other times we would get five hundred to a thousand gems.

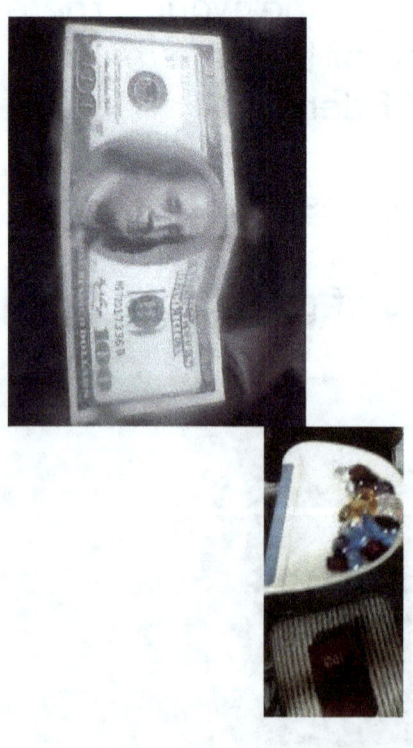

We had people receive $100 Bills in their personal belongings. We even had ten $100 Bills fall during meetings in one weekend. God can cause wealth of the wicked to be released to the righteous. One woman testified that she received one in her purse. Another woman found a $100 Bill in her Bible while at home. You can choose to believe or not to believe that is your choice.

Most ministries that have gemstones come in their meetings refer to the Breastplate. The Breastplate has gemstones in it and they believe God is bringing us gemstones as a sign. This is okay but I want to look deeper. I love to confirm and confirm again.

Isaiah 58:12 And *they that shall be* of thee shall build the old waste places: thou shalt raise up the foundations of many generations; and thou shalt be called, The repairer of the breach, The restorer of paths to dwell in.

God is restoring. I know God is bringing new waves of signs and wonders. What I have seen is just the beginning.

Ezekiel 28:13, 14 Thou hast been in **Eden the garden of God**; every **precious stone** *was* **thy covering, the sardius, topaz, and the diamond, the beryl, the onyx, and the jasper, the sapphire, the emerald, and the carbuncle, and gold**: the workmanship of thy tabrets and of thy pipes was

prepared in thee in the day that thou wast created. Thou *art* the anointed cherub that covereth; and I have set thee *so:* thou wast upon the holy mountain of God; thou hast walked up and down in the midst of the stones of fire.

A Big part of the restoration is from what was in the Garden of Eden. God sent Jesus and we are in the process of seeing the restoration of all that was lost. I believe that the purity, Glory and even gemstones were common in the garden. "On Earth as it is in Heaven" God is bringing the kingdom of Heaven to Earth.

Ezekiel 1:26 And above the firmament that *was* over their heads *was* the likeness of a throne, as the appearance of a sapphire stone: and upon the likeness of the throne *was* the likeness as the appearance of a man above upon it.

Ezekiel 10:1 Then I looked, and, behold, in the firmament that was above the head of the cherubims there appeared over them as it were a sapphire stone, as the appearance of the likeness of a throne.

A lot of people challenge and judge this manifestation more than most. I believe we would see more of these manifestations if we would come in unity. It's time to agree on what we can agree on and press in to the King of Glory.

JESUS

Remember I'm talking about restoration. The wall of the New Jerusalem is part of that.

As God brings things closer to this fulfillment we will see gemstones as a sign from Heaven.

Revelations 21:18-27 And the building of the wall of it was *of* jasper: and the city *was* pure gold, like unto clear glass. And the foundations of the wall of the city *were* garnished with all manner of precious stones. The first foundation *was* jasper; the second, sapphire; the third, a chalcedony;

the fourth, an emerald; The fifth, sardonyx; the sixth, sardius; the seventh, chrysolite; the eighth, beryl; the ninth, a topaz; the tenth, a chrysoprasus; the eleventh, a jacinth; the twelfth, an amethyst. And the twelve gates *were* twelve pearls; every several gate was of one pearl: and the street of the city *was* pure gold, as it were transparent glass. And I saw no temple therein: for the Lord God Almighty and the Lamb are the temple of it. And the city had no need of the sun, neither of the moon, to shine in it: for the glory of God did lighten it, and the Lamb *is* the light thereof. And the nations of them which are saved shall walk in the light of it: and the kings of the earth do bring their glory and honour into it. And the gates of it shall not be shut at all by day: for there shall be no night there. And they shall bring the glory and honour of the nations into it. And there shall in no wise enter into it any thing that defileth, neither *whatsoever* worketh abomination, or *maketh* a lie: but they which are written in the Lamb's book of life.

We need to expect God to do this. Some will go after gemstones but I believe if we go after God first gemstones will follow.

Chapter Seven

Signs Are For Everyone

Signs & Wonders are for everyone. The only requirement is to believe. God is looking for those whom are willing to be a sign and wonder.

Mark 16:17 And these **signs shall follow them that believe**; In my name shall they cast out devils; they shall speak with new tongues;

God showed me something that really blew me away. He showed me something in verse 14.

Mark 16:14 Afterward he appeared unto the eleven as they sat at meat, and **upbraided them with their unbelief and hardness of heart**, because they believed not them which had seen him after he was risen.

Jesus spoke about unbelief and hardness of hearts. We have to think about this. Jesus then tells them that signs follow them that believe. It shows me a picture of the Church today, doubt and unbelief with hard hearts.

Mark 16:19, 20 So then after the Lord had spoken unto them, he was received up into heaven, and

sat on the right hand of God. And they went forth, and preached every where, the Lord working with *them,* and **confirming the word with signs following**. Amen.

Acts 2:41-43 Then they that gladly received his word were baptized: and the same day there were added *unto them* about three thousand souls. And they continued stedfastly in the apostles' doctrine and fellowship, and in breaking of bread, and in prayers. And fear came upon every soul: and **many wonders and signs were done by the apostles**.

Signs and Wonders for Evangelism

The early Church added daily all that were saved. We need to see that in our local Church. A dead Church will not draw the harvest but signs and wonders will.

Acts 5:12 And **by the hands of the apostles were many signs and wonders wrought among the people**; (and they were all with one accord in Solomon's porch.

Acts 5:14 And **believers were the more added to the Lord, multitudes** both of men and women.)

Signs and wonders draw man and women to the feet of Jesus today.

Confirming Scriptures

I want to give all whom read this more scripture about signs and wonders. May God's Glory fall upon you as you read this?

Daniel 4:2 I thought it good to **shew the signs and wonders** that the high God hath wrought toward me.

Daniel 6:27 He delivereth and rescueth, and he **worketh signs and wonders** in heaven and in earth, who hath delivered Daniel from the power of the lions.

Hebrews 2:3, 4 How shall we escape, if we neglect so great salvation; which at the first began to be spoken by the Lord, and was confirmed unto us by them that heard *him;* God also bearing *them* witness, both with **signs and wonders**, and with divers miracles, and gifts of the Holy Ghost, according to his own will?

Isaiah 8:18 Behold, I and the children whom the LORD hath given me *are* for **signs and for wonders** in Israel from the LORD of hosts, which dwelleth in mount Zion.

Acts 2:22 Ye men of Israel, hear these words; Jesus of Nazareth, a man approved of God among you by miracles and **wonders and signs**, which God did by him in the midst of you, as ye yourselves also know:

Deuteronomy 26:8 And the LORD brought us forth out of Egypt with a mighty hand, and with an outstretched arm, and with great terribleness, and with **signs, and with wonders**:

There were signs and wonders that Jesus did. That was never written in the Word of God.

John 20:30, 31 And **many other signs truly did Jesus in the presence of his disciples, which are not written in this book**: But these are written, that ye might believe that Jesus is the Christ, the Son of God; and that believing ye might have life through his name.

John 21:25 And there are also **many other things which Jesus did**, the which, if they should be written every one, I suppose that even the world itself could not contain the books that should be written. Amen.

Chapter Eight

Testimonies

Here are some of the most amazing testimonies of signs and wonders. They have been kept in the form we received them.

A Husband sent this about his wife: "Oh! My wife was flossing her teeth Sunday evening and noticed all her fillings [about 10] had been turned to Gold! She was so on fire and anointed after the meetings. That she even preached an awesome sermon Sunday morning! All glory to King Yeshua!"

Prophetic Word & Testimony 1/23/11: Bill, after hearing your anointed message on Saturday night and discerning that YOU ARE A LEADER OF THIS ILLINOIS REVIVAL as well as the accuracy of your WORDS OF KNOWLEDGE TO THOSE I WAS WITH AND MYSELF FOR AT LEAST A 1/2 HOUR INTERMITTENTLY ABOUT LITERATURE, WRITING BOOKS AND BOOKLETS. without getting you puffed up I will say now that I've heard many words of knowledge from 3 or 4 other men whom I respect greatly, but they weren't so zeroed in as you were the other night ......

Testimony of a man that has been coming to many meetings: During praise and worship yesterday I looked down and found a gem at my feet. God is good! (This was at his Church on Sunday Morning.)

Testimony of a woman that has been coming to a lot of meetings: Hi Bill, I was not able to make it to the meetings this past weekend but I just wanted to tell you that I found a beautiful gemstone in my house last night. It appeared on my bathroom floor.

I had placed a shirt on the floor and then when I bent down to pick the shirt up approximately 5 minutes later it was there next to the shirt. It is so beautiful! Praise God! You had a word about God doings some amazing things in our home and you weren't kidding! God is good. I believe the gemstone in our home is a sign that the Lord truly is doing some amazing things with our family- both physically and spiritually!

Jesse:
Bill, last nights Meeting was AWESOME!!!!!!! The Prophetic word I received was right on target. I needed to hear some things and God went above and beyond what I thought I needed to hear. I am so Blessed by God and your Ministry Bill. Thank you so much for doing what you do. You, my brother are anointed of God and I am blessed to call you my friend. HALLELUJAH!!!!!!! Merry Christmas and Happy BIRTHDAY!!!

Shanna:
Thank you and God bless you for your faithfulness. I know by the Spirit of the Lord that He is

expanding your borders. You will go forth and do what the Lord has set before you to do- you already are. He has much for you. He will always bless you and provide your every need. You will experience a greater level of freedom. I see chains being removed off your ankles. I believe the Lord will reach MANY people through you and not just a few here and here, but MANY! MANY! MANY!

THANK YOU SO MUCH!

Shanna:
Amen and Amen! I prayed this prayer and will continue to pray for you. I already have. I have been praying for you and the ministry since I looked at the website last week. I felt good in my spirit about everything that I read from the website. I feel blessed and know that you have felt like a prisoner and I know nothing from the physical standpoint, and don't want

to know anything from the physical side. I just know that by the spirit.

A dam is about to open up, so get ready! All will be well and I will continue to pray for you.

Lori:
Great and AWESOME Night Bill!!! Thank You for coming our way. You can see people are hungry for the revelation knowledge that comes straight from the throne!!! Thank You for being so obedient!!!!

Jesse: "Revival waves of Glory is riding the wave of the holy ghost! Doing a little surfing last night."

A Young Lady:
I want to encourage you to hold on and keep doing what you do. My life and the lives of many people i care about may have never changed if it wasn't for going there, so please know what a huge

impact you have made on so many people by being obedient to God....

A Young Lady:
God has used you a lot in so many ways, I have grown so much there ....., the prophecies have touched me greatly, I thank God for people who are obedient to God and follow HIS word.

Lori:
I just wanted to let you know that we miss you. Not hearing your sermons straight from the throne room is kinda depressing..... Whatever is going on I believe you are to be where you are at!!! Bill years ago before the signs started showing up I knew you had a special connection with God. All you had to tell me one night at Ramada Inn Meeting was " Lori, God wanted me to tell you Apple Pie", You even said I don't know why I am suppose to tell you this but I was to say it. I have that tape

and I cherish that prophecy as much as all the others. Bill I asked for something to prove that everything that comes through you was HIM and he proved it!!! So when (a son) was missing for a week and you had given a word from God that I have my hand on him and I WON'T LET HIM GO!!! That was the only words that kept me sane and kept my faith strong. It hurts to hear people say things against the signs and wonders and about the prophecies..... I do know that when we were attending PHM this past year and a half that I felt off in a lot of ways and that something was just not right. I am glad that I am not crazy.

I feel God was trying to protect my family and myself. There was a big blockage and I could not get past it for some reason. I know that the signs and wonders are from God because I has never seen green dust SLOWLY APPEAR in someone's hair before. That could not be a trick or illusion; God always has a way to show me that it is HIM and not man that is proving himself to me. And I know this deep in my spirit. (Another son) prophecy is coming to pass about him becoming a math genius. We put him in a different school, a Christian school. We had parent/teacher conferences the other day. His teacher had given him a test to see what level he was at in math, on a scale of 0% to 100% for 3rd grade, he was at 8%. middle of the 1st quarter she tested him again he was up to 38%. At the end of the 1st quarter he is up to 80%. She can not believe how he was progressing by leaps and bounds in math. All I could think of was his prophecy was coming to pass.(a son) prophecy about how fast he was going to be has come to pass. He was always the Anchor (the last man) in the big man race during 7 on 7 competitions for football.

He could either keep the 1st place in the race or catch them up to be 1st. He has been commented on by the coaches at linemen camp and at school that he is the fastest off the line when the ball is snapped. But the greatest testimony that I have is the numerous prophecies about my husband and how he would be a man of God. If anyone knew him back then they would not believe that it could happen. But God is always faithful and Bill I thank you for being Faithful to and for God, because all of these prophecies have come to pass. It may have taken time but they came to pass and that is main reason I am sending this message to you. Keep up all that you are doing you are doing the right things. Remember it was a long hard journey for Katherine Kuhlman also. But she always kept God 1st and for most in her life and she was greatly blessed for that!!! Hope to hear from you soon, your friend in Christ......

Lori:
Bill, I know this to be true, You are doing the right thing Bill Keep the Faith, Keep believing in all the wondrous things are God has shown us and the that greater things are yet to come.

You have stayed so faithful and true to God and doing everything he tells you to do. DON'T EVER GIVE UP!!!! I will make the next meeting I promise!!! Keep your chin up and who cares what the carnal Christians are saying we know what they are up to, to advance themselves and not God's Kingdom......We love You with all our hearts and we will be praying for you that God will show up in a mighty way to shake up a few Houses!!! lol, Love, ...

Rebecca:
I can always say that in the services God has used you in mighty ways and you always pointed us to Jesus! The prophetic gifting in you has been a personal blessing to me and to my family and we have held tightly to the Prophetic words given to us by God thru you. Please keep us posted of your speaking engagements and as the Lord leads - you'll see us again!

A Woman:
Hi Bill, I am soo very happy that you are happy, I always respected you........ You are a highly favored man of God, whatever you are doing, may God richly bless it, you touched our lives in so many great ways, we both really miss you, bye...

Jesse: *..Glory to God Bill! We are happy and excited for your new lease on life and ministry! HALLELUJAH...*

About the Author

Bill Vincent was born 12/25/73 in Illinois. Bill had a lot of challenges as a child. Bill was the teenager parents didn't want their children to hang with. Bill was invited to a prophetic service about 1990 and after he went that was the service that changed his life. Bill was born again and ministered to for the first time. The man that prophesied to Bill that day was Dennis Goodell of International Miracle Ministries. Dennis Goodell has now gone on to be with the Lord.

Bill was a servant to Dennis Goodell for about ten years and had seen and experienced a great deal of miracles. This was the man Bill received an impartation of gifts of the Holy Spirit.

Bill was trained within the Church for many years. Bill's prophetic gift was matured and sharpened. Bill was ordained in 2001 while being a minister within the Church. Bill continued ministering in the Church and other places. In 2004 Bill established a Church in Litchfield, IL.

This ministry traveled as the Lord led. Bill operated in the prophetic with words of knowledge for healing spirit, soul and body. In 2008 Bill was frustrated and sought God for something fresh. After a couple of months God showed up with His mighty presence. August 2008 a Revival started. God's presence got stronger and stronger. After a few months God began to show up with mighty miracles, healing, signs and wonders. The revival continued for over two years. There were many miracles and signs every week. There were testimonies of Cancers healed, tumors removed, arthritis healed and many other creative miracles.

Bill has an accurate prophetic gift, a powerful revelatory preaching anointing with miracles signs and wonders following.

Bill started a ministry after many years of ministry by the name of Revival

Waves of Glory Ministries in 2010. This ministry is a ministry with a fresh vision. God has brought Bill through much adversity. This ministry has had signs and wonders with deep prophetic ministry. Bill is a Prophet of God with a true Apostolic Anointing. Bill has authored many books, established a School of ministry called The School of the Supernatural and created a book publishing company called Revival Waves of Glory Books & Publishing.

Bill has found the glory of God in an awesome way. He has a special relationship with the father and powerful revelatory, healing and prophetic anointings.

Bill is married to his wife Tabitha who has two beautiful daughters. Bill and his family live in Litchfield, IL. Tabitha works closely with Bill in all the ministries day to day duties. I (Bill Vincent) am grateful every day to have these three amazing women in my life. Thank You Lord!

Recommended Books

By Bill Vincent
Overcoming Obstacles
Glory: Pursuing God's Presence
Defeating the Demonic Realm
Increasing Your Prophetic Gift
Increasing Your Anointing
Keys to Receiving Your Miracle
The Supernatural Realm
Waves of Revival
Increase of Revelation and Restoration
The Resurrection Power of God
Discerning Your Call of God
Apostolic Breakthrough
Increasing God's Glory
Love is Waiting – Don't Let Love Pass You By
The Healing Power of God
Expanding God's Glory
Receiving Personal Prophecy
Signs and Wonders
Signs and Wonders Revelations
Children Stories
I Married Jezebel
Rapture Revelations
The Secret Place of God's Power

Signs and Wonders Revelations

By Bill Vincent Spanish & French Translation
Love is Waiting – Don't Let Love Pass You By
Signs and Wonders Revelations
I Married Jezebel
Increasing Your Prophetic Gift
Receiving Personal Prophecy

By Bill Vincent, Paula Loveless, Joseph Basurto, Dawn Vitale and Jackie Money
Experience God's Love

By Bishop Gregory Leachman
God's Greatest Challenge:
Man & His Ungodly Ways
&
Conforming to the Mind of Christ

By Richard Money
My Life in a Salami Factory

To Order:

Email:
billvincent@revivalwavesofglory.com

Web Site:
www.revivalwavesofglory.com

Mail Order:
Revival Waves of Glory
PO Box 596
Litchfield, IL 62056
Shipping $5.00

Prices do not include shipping and are subject to change. If you mail an order and pay by check, make check out to Revival Waves of Glory.

www.ingramcontent.com/pod-product-compliance
Lightning Source LLC
Chambersburg PA
CBHW072111290426
44110CB00014B/1886